PHONICS CONNECTIONS

The World of Maps

by Wiley Blevins

Table of Contents

capstone classroom

World at a Glance

The world is filled with amazing places. We can't always travel to every city, state, or country. So how can we learn about different places?

A map is one way to learn about the world. A map is a drawing that shows where places are located. A map can show the shape of the land, such as the shape of a state. Maps can also show roads, lakes, rivers, and cities.

Most maps are flat. A globe is different. A globe is a ball-shaped map. It is shaped like Earth. Spinning a globe can help you see the whole world at a glance.

Reading a Map

Let's look at a map of the world. The map on page 5 shows what the world would look like if it were flat.

What does a map have that can help you read it? A map has a key. The map key has symbols, or small drawings. Each symbol represents an object or a place. For example, the color green shows where land is located. The color blue stands for water.

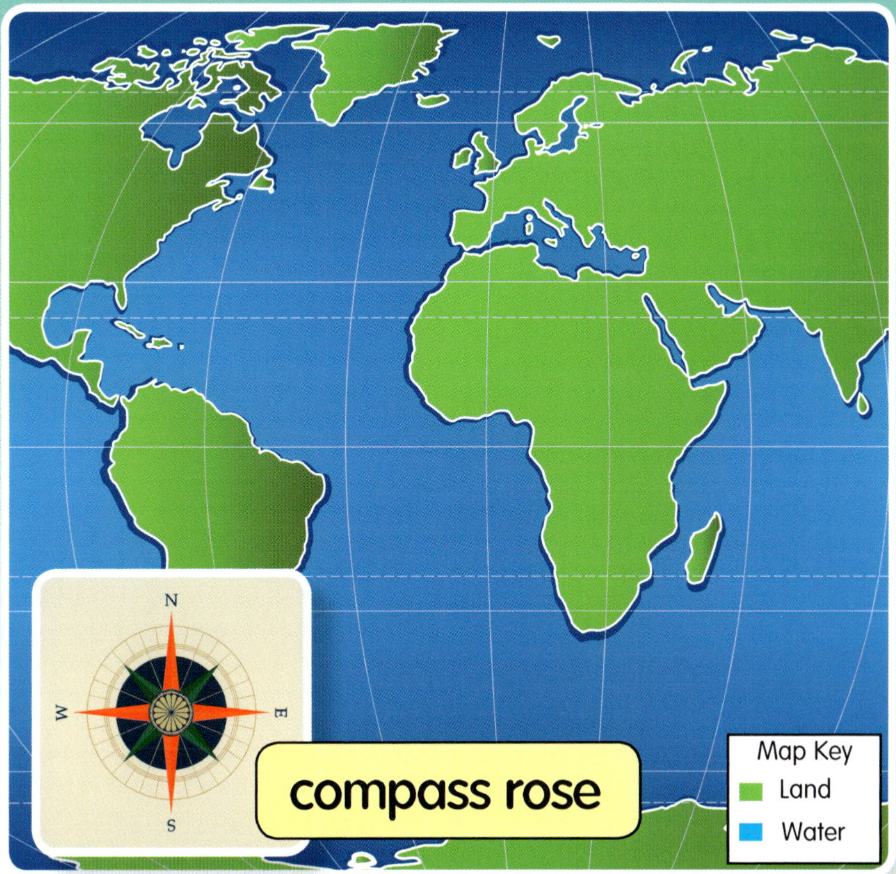

This map also has a compass rose. The compass rose has four points—North, South, East, and West. These are the directions that help you know where you are or where you are going.

A map also has lines to help us find places. For example, the line on a map that splits Earth in half is called the equator. If you trace this line with your finger, you will go all the way around the world.

Half of Earth is above the equator. The other half of Earth is below it. Places that are on or near the equator are usually very hot. The farther you go north or south from the equator, the colder it gets.

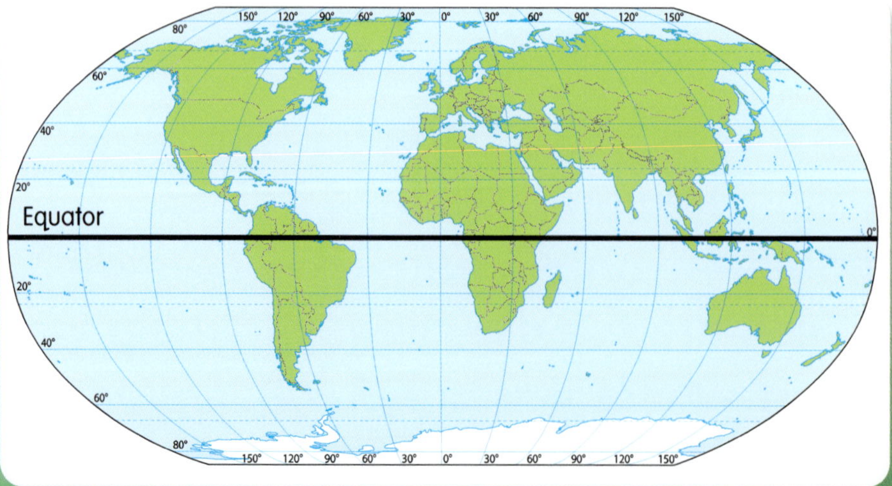

See if you can find the equator on this globe. The United States is located above, or to the north of, the equator.

The Land

Earth is covered by land and water. The land is divided into seven continents. Asia is the continent with the most land and the most people.

map of Asia

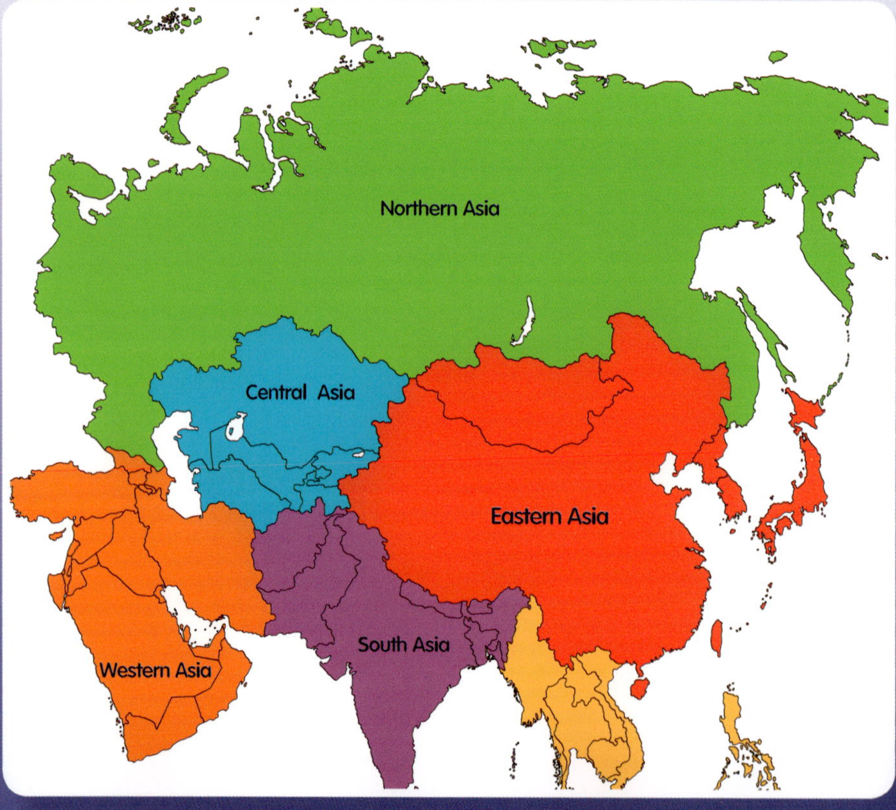

the seven continents of the world

Most of the continents are divided into smaller countries. There are more than 190 countries in the world. The United States is a country. It is located on the continent of North America.

The land on the seven continents differs from place to place. Some places have mountains. Other places have deserts. The land can be flat, grassy, rocky, or filled with forests.

Deserts are hot, dry places. The biggest desert in the world is the Sahara Desert. It is located in the northern part of Africa.

The Water

Earth's water is found mostly in oceans, seas, lakes, rivers, streams, and ponds. On most maps or globes, the color blue is used to show the areas of water.

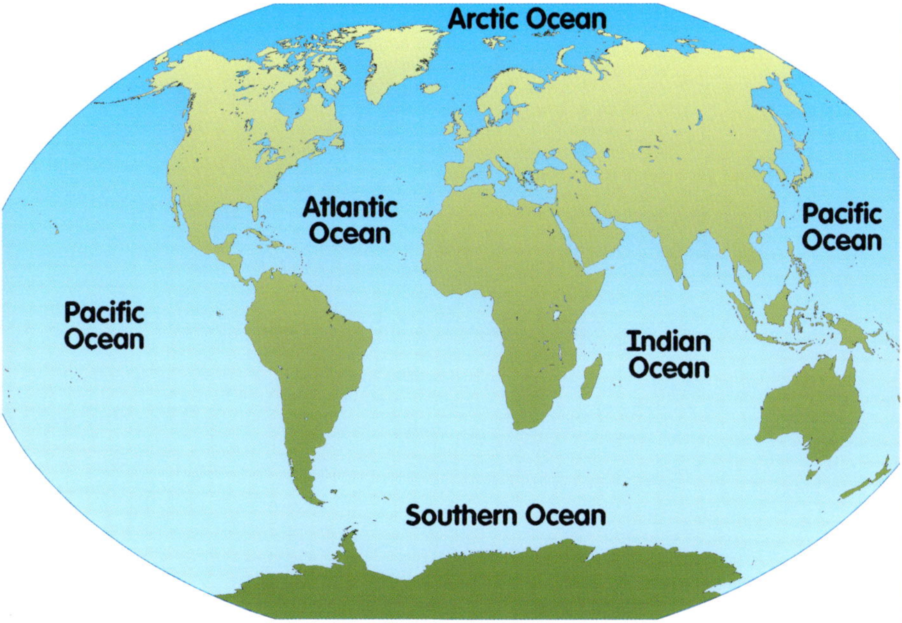

five main oceans

There are five big oceans—the Pacific Ocean, the Atlantic Ocean, the Indian Ocean, the Arctic Ocean, and the Southern Ocean. See if you can find the five oceans on the map.

Lake Superior

Lakes are smaller bodies of water than oceans. The United States has five big lakes. These lakes are called the Great Lakes.

Rivers flow in many places. One of the world's longest rivers is the Amazon River. It is located in South America.

The world is a big and exciting place. You can learn a lot about Earth just by looking at a map.

Index